AF668467

Book Title: **Creative and Innovative Diamond Designs Vol. 2**

ISBN: 978-93-5975-840-4

GTIN (Barcode): 8906104442239

Series: KNOWLEDGE IN MY VEINS ®

Published & promoted by: GURMEETWEB TECHNICAL LABS®

Digital store: https://store.gurmeetweb.com
OTT QUEST™ (OTT Platform): https://ott.quest
SIR QUEST™ (Online Courses): https://sir.quest
Gifs: https://wingift.quest
Web portal: https://gurmeetweb.com

E-mail: contact@gurmeetweb.com

Social Media:

Instagram: https://www.instagram.com/gurmeetweb
Facebook: https://www.facebook.com/GWTLABS
Twitter: https://twitter.com/gurmeetweb
Youtube Channel: https://www.youtube.com/@gurmeetweb

Note: "Creative and Innovative Diamond Designs Vol. 2" Book is created by GURMEET SINGH DANG using Artificial Intelligence (AI), DALL·E 3 and ChatGPT etc. and published and promoted by GURMEETWEB TECHNICAL LABS® which is a sole proprietary firm/company of GURMEET SINGH DANG.

For accessing or utilizing the high-resolution AI images, kindly visit: https://store.gurmeetweb.com

Embark on a captivating journey through the world of luxurious jewelry with "Creative and Innovative Diamond Designs Vol. 2." This exquisite volume is a treasure trove of the most splendid and innovative diamond jewelry pieces, each crafted with meticulous attention to detail and artistic flair. From the classic elegance of Diamond and Sapphire Halo Stud Earrings to the bold and modern Angular Diamond Cuff Bracelet, this book presents a diverse collection of designs that cater to all tastes and occasions.

Each section of the book delves into the unique characteristics and craftsmanship of various pieces, such as the Romantic Rose-Cut Diamond Engagement Ring set in Rose Gold, showcasing vintage charm, and the Chic Diamond Cluster Stud Earrings in Yellow Gold, offering dazzling simplicity. For those who favor a touch of color, the Elegant Diamond and Opal Drop Earrings set in White Gold or the Whimsical Diamond and Moonstone Ring reveal the seamless integration of vibrant gemstones with the timeless sparkle of diamonds.

"Creative and Innovative Diamond Designs Vol. 2" not only serves as a catalog of beautiful jewelry but also as an inspiration for designers and connoisseurs alike. It explores the interplay of different metals, the innovative use of settings, and the artistic incorporation of colored gemstones alongside diamonds to create pieces that are both breathtaking and unique.

Perfect for both industry professionals and jewelry lovers, this book is a must-have for anyone passionate about the art of jewelry design. It promises to inspire and enchant with its detailed descriptions and beautiful imagery, making it an invaluable addition to any collection.

The Book is created by GURMEET SINGH DANG using Artificial Intelligence (AI), DALL-E 3 and ChatGPT etc. This Book is published & promoted by GURMEETWEB TECHNICAL LABS® which is a sole proprietary firm/company of GURMEET SINGH DANG.

Contents

Stud earrings feature a stunning blue sapphire center, encircled by a halo of meticulously selected diamonds, set in a design that exudes classic elegance

The contrast of the deep blue sapphire against the clear diamonds creates a captivating visual effect, making these earrings a perfect choice for those seeking timeless beauty. The halo setting not only enhances the sapphire's vibrancy but also adds an extra layer of sparkle, suitable for both everyday elegance and special occasions.

Bangle bracelet is a celebration of modern luxury, featuring a surface entirely adorned with sparkling pavé-set diamonds

The warm hue of the rose gold complements the brilliance of the diamonds, creating a dazzling effect that catches the eye. Designed for those who appreciate a bold statement in their jewelry, this bracelet is perfect for adding a touch of glamour to any outfit. Its secure clasp ensures that it remains comfortably on the wrist, making it a stunning and practical addition to any jewelry collection.

Sculptural diamond ring is a work of art, designed to make a bold statement

Set in rich yellow gold, its unique, flowing design gracefully wraps around the finger, adorned with diamonds that add a radiant sparkle. The ring's distinctive shape and the interplay of light on its surface make it a captivating piece, ideal for those looking to express their individuality through their jewelry. It embodies a perfect harmony of artistic design and luxurious materials, making it a standout addition to any collection.

Necklace reinterprets the classic Byzantine chain with a luxurious twist, integrating sparkling diamonds into its intricate, interlocking links

Crafted in 14k gold, the necklace exudes a warm glow, enhancing the brilliance of the embedded diamonds. Its complex weave symbolizes strength and eternity, making it more than just a piece of jewelry—it's a statement of enduring elegance. Perfect for adding a sophisticated touch to any outfit, it's a versatile piece that bridges the gap between traditional craftsmanship and contemporary luxury.

These drop earrings showcase the ethereal beauty of opals, complemented by the timeless sparkle of diamonds

Set in sleek white gold, the opals' play of color is accentuated against the light, creating a captivating visual effect. The diamonds add a layer of sophistication, making these earrings a perfect choice for those who seek elegance with a hint of mystery. Whether worn at a gala or a intimate dinner, they promise to draw admiration and elevate any ensemble.

Cuff bracelet presents a bold, modern design with its angular lines and a surface adorned with sparkling diamonds

Crafted in sterling silver, the bracelet offers a contemporary twist on classic elegance, making it a striking accessory for the modern woman. Its open cuff design ensures a comfortable fit, while the diamonds catch the light, adding brilliance to any movement. Perfect for those who appreciate jewelry that makes a statement, this piece combines sophistication with a modern edge.

Engagement ring features a rose-cut diamond, known for its flat bottom and domed top, which maximizes the stone's brilliance

Set in romantic rose gold, the ring's vintage charm is accentuated, offering a timeless symbol of love. The unique cut of the diamond, paired with the warm hues of rose gold, creates an enchanting piece that's perfect for those who cherish the beauty of bygone eras. It's an ideal expression of commitment for those seeking a ring as unique as their love story.

Diamond Riviera necklace is the epitome of sophistication, featuring a continuous line of perfectly matched diamonds

This classic piece illuminates the neckline with unparalleled brilliance, making it a statement of elegance and luxury. Ideal for special occasions, the necklace complements any formal attire, adding a touch of timeless glamour. Its seamless design and exquisite craftsmanship ensure it remains a cherished piece in any jewelry collection, symbolizing the pinnacle of refined taste.

Earrings combine the timeless allure of diamonds with the boldness of black onyx, set in a geometric design that's both striking and contemporary

The stark contrast between the sparkling diamonds and the deep, matte finish of the onyx creates a captivating visual effect, while the sterling silver setting adds a sleek, modern finish. Perfect for those who embrace bold styles, these earrings are a statement piece that can elevate any look, offering a blend of sophistication and avant-garde design.

Ring showcases the ethereal beauty of moonstone, complemented by the timeless sparkle of diamonds

Set in durable platinum, the ring features a central moonstone known for its enchanting play of light and color. The flanking diamonds enhance the moonstone's natural allure, creating a piece that seems almost magical. Ideal for those who appreciate jewelry with a story or a touch of whimsy, this ring combines the best of elegance and enchantment, making it a unique addition to any collection.

Pendant necklace draws inspiration from vintage designs, featuring a vibrant peridot surrounded by a halo of sparkling diamonds

The classic setting, combined with the bright green hue of the peridot, offers a look of timeless elegance with a delightful pop of color. Set in a fine metal that complements both the diamonds and the peridot, this piece is perfect for those who love vintage style but desire a touch of modern vibrancy. It's an ideal accessory for adding sophistication and a hint of color to any ensemble.

Stud earrings feature a cluster of brilliantly cut diamonds, set in warm yellow gold

The arrangement of the diamonds creates a dazzling effect, mimicking the sparkle of a much larger stone. The yellow gold setting adds a classic touch, ensuring these earrings provide an elegant look suitable for both day and night. Crafted for those who appreciate subtle luxury, these studs are a versatile addition to any jewelry collection, offering timeless elegance with a contemporary flair.

Bracelet combines the serene beauty of aquamarine with the subtle sparkle of diamonds, set in a delicate white gold chain

The soft blue hue of the aquamarine offers a tranquil hint of color, complemented by the diamonds' light-catching properties. Perfect for those who prefer their jewelry to convey understated elegance, this bracelet is versatile enough to wear daily, adding a touch of calm beauty to any outfit. It exemplifies simplicity and grace, making it a cherished piece for any occasion.

Ring features an exquisite marquise diamond, known for its boat-like shape that maximizes carat weight and brilliance

The diamond is set in a modern, minimalistic band that enhances its natural beauty without overwhelming it. This piece combines the timeless appeal of a solitaire diamond with contemporary design elements, making it an ideal choice for those seeking a standout engagement ring or a statement piece for special occasions. The sleek setting highlights the diamond's unique shape, offering a sophisticated and bold aesthetic.

Ring elegantly pairs a richly hued garnet with a circle of sparkling diamonds, creating a stunning halo effect

Set in 18k gold, the warmth of the metal beautifully complements the deep red of the garnet, while the surrounding diamonds add a touch of vintage glamour. Ideal for those who appreciate jewelry with a story and depth, this piece draws inspiration from classic designs but is crafted for the modern wearer. The combination of garnet and diamond evokes a sense of timeless romance, making it a perfect gift or a treasured addition to any collection.

Threader earrings redefine modern elegance with their unique design and the subtle sparkle of diamonds

Set in white gold, the earrings offer a minimalist yet edgy aesthetic, perfect for those who love contemporary jewelry. The threader style allows for a dynamic movement, with diamonds that catch the light beautifully, providing just the right amount of shimmer. Versatile and sophisticated, these earrings are suited for daily wear or special occasions, adding a modern twist to any ensemble.

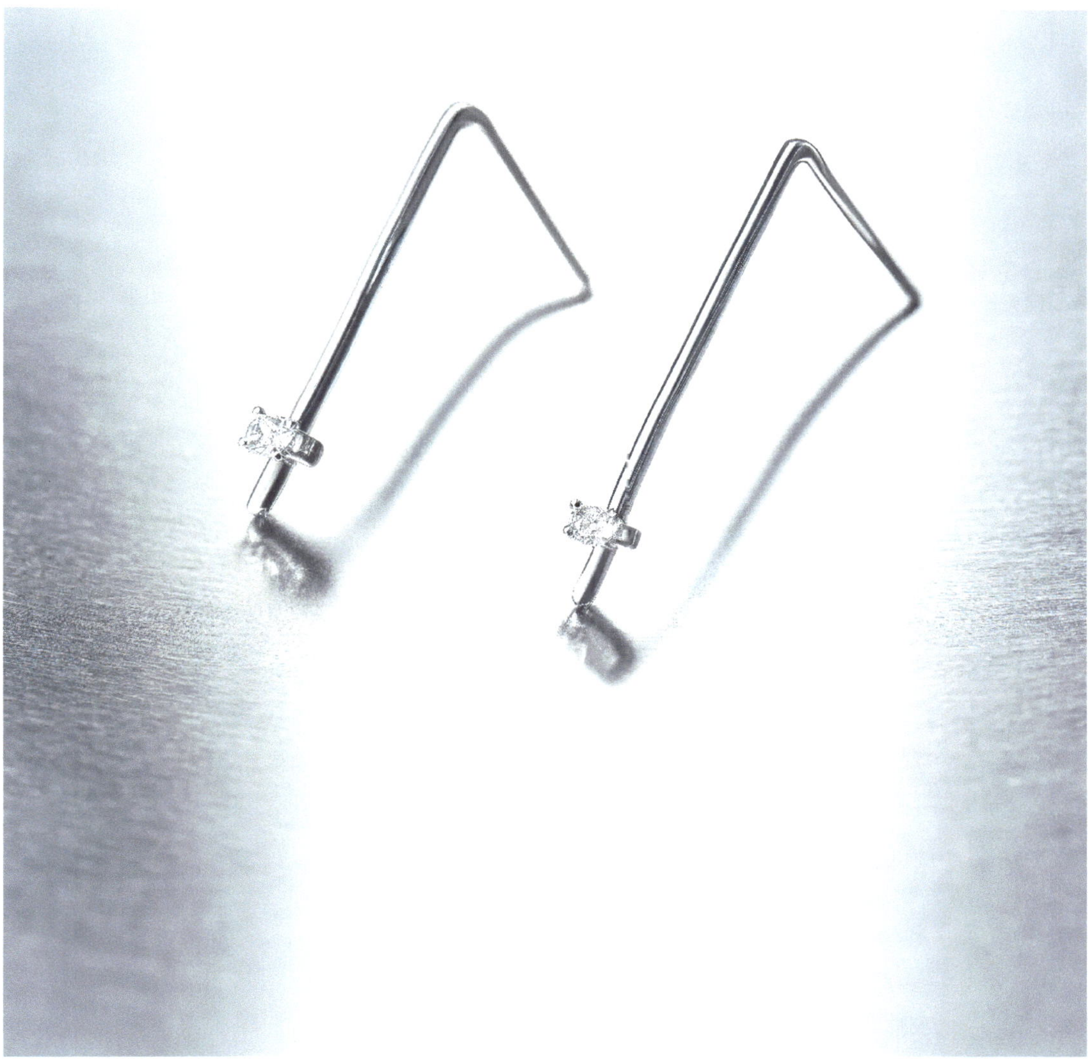

Brooch pays homage to the Art Nouveau era, known for its emphasis on organic forms and flowing lines

It beautifully combines sparkling diamonds with deep purple amethyst, set in a design that mimics natural motifs. The contrast between the bright sparkle of the diamonds and the rich hue of the amethyst creates a piece that is both striking and elegant. Perfect for adding a touch of luxury and historical charm to any outfit, this brooch is a testament to timeless design and exquisite craftsmanship, appealing to those who appreciate artistry in their jewelry.

Necklace features a key pendant, a symbol of mystery and discovery, adorned with delicate diamonds that add a touch of elegance and light

Set in rose gold, the pendant combines the warmth of the metal with the brilliance of the diamonds, creating a piece that's both meaningful and stylish. The key motif makes it a thoughtful gift or personal keepsake, symbolizing the unlocking of new beginnings or hidden secrets. Perfect for everyday wear or as a special accessory, this necklace brings a hint of romance and intrigue to any collection.

Engagement ring centers around a stunning cushion-cut diamond, known for its soft corners and deep brilliance

The solitaire setting in polished platinum elevates the diamond's natural beauty, offering a timeless symbol of love and commitment. The cushion cut combines the best of classic and modern styles, making it an ideal choice for those seeking a ring that is both elegant and enduring. Its refined simplicity ensures it will remain a cherished piece for generations, symbolizing a lasting bond.

Diamond ear jackets present a contemporary take on classic ear jewelry

Crafted in radiant yellow gold and adorned with sparkling diamonds, they offer a bold, modern aesthetic. The unique design wraps around the earlobe, creating an illusion of floating diamonds that catch the light from every angle. Perfect for the fashion-forward individual, these ear jackets provide a striking balance between avant-garde design and timeless elegance, making them a standout addition to any jewelry collection.

Diamond bar necklace, with its sleek design and lustrous white gold setting, embodies modern minimalism

The straight bar pendant is studded with diamonds, providing a subtle yet striking sparkle. Its simplicity and elegance make it ideal for layering with other necklaces or wearing on its own for a minimalist statement. Versatile and chic, it complements any outfit, making it a staple piece for those who appreciate contemporary jewelry that offers both style and sophistication.

Brooch brings the playful elegance of a butterfly to life, adorned with sparkling diamonds and vibrant gemstone accents

Set in a fine metal framework, the brooch showcases a variety of colors, mirroring the natural beauty of butterflies. Its whimsical design does not sacrifice luxury, making it a perfect piece for those who love to blend playfulness with sophistication. Whether worn on a lapel, scarf, or hat, this brooch adds a touch of whimsy and color, appealing to those who cherish nature-inspired jewelry with a luxurious twist.

Tennis bracelet combines the brilliance of diamonds with the rich green of emeralds, set in a seamless white gold chain

The alternating pattern of gemstones creates a harmonious balance of color and sparkle, making it an exquisite piece of jewelry that radiates timeless elegance. Perfect for special occasions or adding a sophisticated touch to everyday attire, this bracelet is a versatile addition to any jewelry collection. It embodies the blend of luxury and classic style, appealing to those who appreciate the beauty of traditional gemstones in a contemporary setting.

Two-finger diamond ring in white gold is a testament to modern jewelry design, offering a unique and bold statement

The sleek white gold band elegantly extends across two fingers, adorned with brilliant diamonds that add sparkle and sophistication. Its distinctive style makes it a perfect choice for those who seek to stand out and express their individuality through their accessories. Combining contemporary design with timeless elegance, this ring is a captivating addition to any fashion-forward jewelry collection.

Cocktail ring showcases a stunning blue topaz center stone, encapsulated by sparkling diamonds and set in luxurious yellow gold

The vibrant blue of the topaz contrasts beautifully with the warm gold and the bright diamonds, creating a piece that is both eye-catching and sophisticated. Ideal for special occasions or as a statement piece in a jewelry collection, this ring combines the allure of fine gemstones with exquisite craftsmanship, making it a symbol of elegance and refined taste.

Station necklace in rose gold captivates with its simplicity and elegance

Featuring bezel-set diamonds evenly spaced along a delicate chain, it offers a subtle sparkle that enhances any outfit. The warm hue of the rose gold perfectly complements the brilliance of the diamonds, making this necklace a versatile and timeless piece. Whether worn alone or layered with other necklaces, it adds a touch of sophistication to both casual and formal attire, embodying minimalist elegance at its finest.

Watch bracelet draws inspiration from the geometric elegance of the Art Deco period, featuring a harmonious blend of sparkling diamonds and vivid sapphires

The piece not only serves as a functional timepiece but also as a statement of timeless style. Set in fine metal, the combination of gemstones and Art Deco-inspired design elements makes it a unique accessory that stands out for its beauty and craftsmanship. Ideal for those who appreciate the allure of vintage jewelry and the elegance of historical design periods, this watch bracelet is a celebration of past and present.

Flower ring, set in rose gold, is a delightful expression of nature's beauty, featuring petals adorned with pink sapphires and a center of sparkling diamonds

The warm rose gold setting enhances the pink hues of the sapphires, while the diamonds add a touch of brilliance, creating a piece that is both playful and elegant. Perfect for those who love jewelry that tells a story or captures the essence of nature, this ring is a vibrant addition to any collection, symbolizing growth, beauty, and the joy of life.

Eternity band elevates the concept of timeless elegance with its sleek design, showcasing a continuous circle of baguette-cut diamonds set in lustrous platinum

The straight edges of the baguette diamonds offer a modern and sophisticated aesthetic, making it an ideal choice for those who appreciate contemporary design. The platinum setting ensures durability and a bright, reflective surface that enhances the diamonds' natural brilliance. This ring is a perfect symbol of everlasting love, combining luxury with a modern sensibility.

Pendant features a masterful display of filigree work in antique silver, embellished with tiny diamonds that sparkle within the intricate designs

The vintage-inspired piece captures the elegance and craftsmanship of a bygone era, making it a unique addition to any jewelry collection. Ideal for those who cherish the beauty of antique jewelry, this pendant necklace combines the old-world charm of filigree with the timeless appeal of diamonds, offering a piece that's both historical and elegant.

www.ingramcontent.com/pod-product-compliance
Lightning Source LLC
Chambersburg PA
CBHW041528180726
48282CB00053B/114
9789359758404